Growing Your Ministry God's Way

WORKBOOK

(Using Your Spiritual Gifts)

Gertrude Joanne Pollard- Watts

ISBN 978-0-578-45317-0

Copyright © 2019 by Gertrude Joanne Pollard-Watts

All rights reserved. No part of this publication may be reproduced, distributed, or transmitted in any form or by any means, including photocopying, recording, or other electronic or mechanical methods without the prior written permission of the publisher. For permission request, solicit the publisher via the email address below.

Gertrude Joanne Pollard- Watts

5036 Hardy McManus Road

Evans, Georgia 30809

Email: gjpwatts.teach@gmail.com

Printed in the United States of America

"For God so loved the world that he gave his one and only Son, that whoever believes in him shall not perish but have eternal life," (John 3:16; NIV)

Contents

Thank you, God... 6

A word from the Instructor......................................8

Introduction..10

Work Syllabus..11

Lessons...11

Supplies/ Resources.. 12

Instructions for Completing Assignments..................14

Week 1 Why God Gives Spiritual Gifts....................15

Week 2 Recognizing Your Spiritual Gifts.................19

Week 3 Understanding What Spiritual Gifts Entail.........22

Week 4 Continuation/ Understanding What Spiritual Gifts Entail..26

Week 5 How to Use Your Spiritual Gifts God's Way and Reap a Harvest in Your Ministry....................30

Week 6 How to Sustain Your Ministry......................35

Week 7 A Blessed Ministry Brings Forth Growth in the Church...38

Week 8 Thanking God in All Thing.........................42

Week 9 Assay..45

Seek-N- Find/Match Games...................................47

Conclusion..51

Blessing Others..…......52

Growing Your Ministry God's Way Workbook Lessons/
    Answer Sheet…..53

Match Game/ Answer Sheet...…..............................65

End of Course Questionnaire..................................66

About the Author..................................….......68

Thank You God

Thank You God for the love, mercy, grace, protection and favor you are giving me throughout life. I thank you for accepting me into your family in Christ Jesus and using me for your glory. Thank you for continuing to guide me with your words, instructions wisdom, knowledge, and understanding, and giving me the strength and obedience in following you Jesus. I recognize sometimes I have fallen short, but you allow me to repent and get back on the right track. Thank You my Heavenly Father, for supplying all my needs accordingly to your riches and glory and allowing me to write this workbook by the guidance of your Holy Spirit and allowing the anointing of your words to manifest in the lives of all who read and complete it all over the world. Now Lord I am asking you to allow your anointing to also enrich their lives with your wisdom, knowledge, and understanding not only be a blessing to them but also into the kingdom of the Lord Jesus… And thank you God, for continuing to reveal to me your destiny for my life, as scripture says in (Jeremiah 29:11, NIV) "For I know the plans I have for you, declares the LORD, plans to prosper you and not to harm you, plans to give you hope and a future."

A Word from the Instructor

Hi, my name is Gertrude Watts and welcome to the workbook course of "Growing Your Ministry God's Way: Using Your Spiritual Gifts. I am so excited for you and wishing you a fulfilling success in completing this Workbook! Theology has always been my passion and I'm honored to share the things I have learned with you, so you can continue to grow in the ways of God, while being encouraged to use your Spiritual gift/s to Grow Your Ministry God's way.

As we adventure into God's words through biblical reading, discussion questions, sharing, and many other forms of studying and learning, one will see how the Word of God can truly make an impact in the lives of people. As a witness I can certainly say it has made an impact in my life in so many ways! Others has also witness to me how the word of God came alive in their lives and changed them or their circumstances. So, while completing this workbook you will get a chance to read about how God made in impact in the lives of people, and hear testimonies from family, friends and church members along the way!

I have been studying and teaching the word of God for many years and still enjoyed every minute of it! As a servant of God, I have had the opportunity to serve in different ministries in the church, but what also gives me great joy is hearing from others what God allowed me to share with others made an impact in their lives and ministry. So hopefully I will have the same opportunity to hear such feedback from you as well. Again, I wish you the very best in this workbook, and in all your endeavors. May God bless you!

Words of Encouragement: Colossians 3:23-24 "Whatever you do, work at it with all your heart, as working for the Lord, not for men, since you know that you will receive an inheritance from the Lord as a reward. It is the Lord Christ you are serving."

Introduction

Growing Your Ministry God's Way Workbook: Using Your Spiritual Gifts is a workbook that is based on the Word of God and has been guided by the Holy Spirit while being developed. As one adventures into the Word of God through Biblical Readings, Assignments, Discussion Questions, Sharing, Test taking, and many other forms of studying; one will learn the importance of why God gives Spiritual gifts, how to recognize your Spiritual gifts and the importance of using your Spiritual gifts as a tool in having a successful ministry.

Growing Your Ministry God's Way Workbook: Using Your Spiritual Gifts also brings out examples of biblical characters praying, showing love, having compassion, forgiveness, and serving others. This workbook also brings out the importance of having faith in God and allowing the Holy Spirit to be your guide in your ministry. But, that's not all! Growing Your Ministry God's Way Workbook: Using Your Spiritual Gifts also teaches the Word of God through Seek-N-Find, Match Games, and Fill in the Blanks Questions!

So, while going on an adventure through studying, learning, and applying the Word of God in your ministry and your life, don't forget to make disciples in the process. May God continue to bless you and your ministry.

*Note: This Workbook can be used in all Ministries of the Church.

Workbook Syllabus

Objectives

- Main objective- is to teach through reading the Word of God, discussing, sharing, test taking, etc. and applying biblical concepts and principles to your life
- Learn how to grow your Ministry God's Way through Faith, the Word of God, and applying life application
- Learning the importance of Spiritual Gifts
- Learning how to Recognize Your Spiritual Gift/s
- Understand What Spiritual Gifts Entail
- Teach how to Use Your Spiritual Gift/s God's Way and Reap a Harvest in Your Ministry
- Teach how to Sustain Your Ministry
- Tcach how a blessed ministry brings forth growth in the church
- Teach the Importance of Thanking God in All Thing
- Giving Words of Encouragement along the way.

Workbook Lessons

Lesson 1 Why God Gives Spiritual Gifts

Lesson 2 Recognizing Your Spirit Gift/s

Lesson 3 Understanding What Spiritual Gifts Entail

Lesson 4 Continues in the 4th Week (Understanding What Spiritual Gifts Entails)

Lesson 5 How to Use Your Spiritual Gift/s God's Way and Reap a Harvest in Your Ministry

Lesson 6 How to Sustain Your Ministry

Lesson 7 A Bless Ministry Brings Forth Growth in the Church according to the Will of God

Lesson 8 Thinking God in All Things

Lesson 9 Conclusion and End of Course Questionnaire

- Write a 250 Word Assay telling how this course will benefit you in your ministry
- Complete the End of course questionnaire (Critiquing the workbook)

Workbook Supplies and Resources

- <u>Recommended</u>: Life Application Study Bible, New International Version (NIV), or the Scofield Study Bible- NIV. These versions will be used by the instructor... BUT other versions can be used, just note that the wordings could be a little different.
- <u>Book</u>- Growing Your Ministry God's Way: Using Your Spiritual Gifts- Author: Gertrude Joanne Pollard-Watts
- <u>Workbook</u>- Growing Your Ministry God's Way: Using Your Spiritual Gifts- Author:
- Gertrude Joanne Pollard Watts.

- A family member, friend or church member you can go to for discussion and share time
- Notice: Books used in connection with the course may be subject to copyright protection.

*Notice: Only "Growing Your Ministry God's Way: Using Your Spiritual Gifts" can be purchased in the form of a book and e-book.

Note: Suppliers

- Book can be purchased at walmart.com, amazon.com and barnsandnoble.com also other online bookstores where available.
- Workbook can be purchased at amazon.com and barnsandnoble.com and look for it to be sold at other online bookstores including at walmart.com
- https://www.kobo.com/us/en/ebook/growing-your-ministry-god-s-way

*Instructions for Completing Assignments

<u>Reading and other Assignments</u> - Below is a format to follow in completing this workbook and instructions when assignments are to be completed. This format is not written in stone! One can also implement their own plans in completing this workbook or follow their Ministry leader's guidelines in completing the assignments

- Assignments will be given the first day of every week (Monday) and will be expected to be completed by Friday of every week.
- Discussion Questions (DQ) at least 150 words each, must be completed by Wednesday of each week.
- Test should be taken on Friday of every week and can be checked by the answer sheet in the back of the workbook when completed.
- Share time (writing assignments/ sharing with a family member, friend or church member) must be completed by Friday of each week

Using Your Spiritual Gifts

Lesson 1

Reading Assignment (Week 1) "Why God Gives Spiritual Gift/s"

- Book- Growing Your Ministry God's Way: Using Your Spiritual Gifts, read pages 11-13 and meditate on these pages.
- Study Bible- Write down three Scriptures about love and explain.
- Read the book of Daniel-Chapter 6.

Discussion Questions   Must be completed by Wednesday of each week.

1. DQ should be at least 150 words each.
2. What was Daniel's spiritual gift?
3. In your reading of Daniel 6, write then discuss with a family member, friend, or church member why Daniel kept praying and was so sure that God would deliver him from the lion's den. Complete your answer by Wednesday of week 1.

Notice: When completing DQ's it must be done in a Mature and Respectful way.

Share time

In the book of Daniel chapter 6 write at least 150 words essay and share with a family member, friend, or church member how the love of God will never fail when we put our faith in him just like Daniel.

Reflection

- In this session the topic that we're going to go over is "Why God gives Spiritual gift/s." In this week reading assignment it talks about things such as love, faith, some knowing their spiritual gift's and using them, and in the mist pointing people to Jesus Christ, and others being afraid of using their spiritual gift/s and letting them become idle in the mist. But we certainly cannot say that about Daniel! Christian's in modern day time have got to be just as faithful in using their spiritual gift/s as Daniel. Even though Daniel faced challenging circumstances he remained faithful in trusting God for his deliverance. And, what about the outcome... not only did God showed his unfailing love to Daniel but in Daniel 6:20-28 God sent his angel to deliver him from the lion's den! Other things happened too! King Darius saw that Daniel, servant of the true living God was innocent, and the king had the men who falsely accused him thrown into the lions' den along with their wives and children; and all their bones were crushed!
- King Darius was shown the glory of God and his heart was touched and he became a believer of the

God Daniel served to the point ...he wrote to all the peoples, nations and men of every language throughout the land: "May you prosper greatly!" I issue a decree that in every part of my kingdom people must fear and reverence the God of Daniel. "For he is the living God and he endures forever; his kingdom will not be destroyed, his dominion will never end. He rescues and saves; he performs signs and wonders in the heavens and on the earth. He rescued Daniel from the power of the lions." So, Daniel prosed during the reign of Darius and the reign of Darius and Persian.

Words of encouragement: "Commit you way to the Lord; trust in him, and he will do this: He will make your righteousness shine like the dawn, the justice of your cause like the noonday sun." Psalm 37:5

Using Your Spiritual Gifts

* This week's quiz will be focused on "The Introduction and Why God Gives Spiritual Gifts." Questions will be taken from your readings and will be given in a way that will allow one to think about the importance of why God bless his children with Spiritual Gifts. And, applying the concepts into ones' ministry in faith, and allowing God to grow their ministry.

Lesson 1   Note: All Quizzes are due by Friday of every Week

Week 1- Quiz

1. What is the foundation of having a successful ministry?

2. In your reading assignment give two scriptures that are related to your answer to the first question.
3. T/F God does not want you to pray to him for a successful ministry.

4. It is impossible to please God without what?

5. Where can you find this scripture in the Bible?

6. In your readings (Daniel 6), what did Daniel refuse to do that got him thrown into the lion's den?

7. What did Daniel do in faith and put his trust in?

8. What was the decree that Daniel refused to obey?

9. Do Christians have to follow the ways of ungodly leaders in the modern- day churches? Why or why not?

10. Where do Spiritual gifts come from?

11. Can you have more than one Spiritual gift?

12. Why does God give Spiritual Gifts?

13. Are all Spiritual gifts in the Church in modern day time being used? Explain your answer

14. What are your Spiritual gift/s? If you don't know just put don't know for your answer.

15. T/F God blesses his children' so they can always have enough for themselves only.

Using Your Spiritual Gifts

Lesson 2

*Note: Please look back at the Course Syllabus and follow the instructions for all guidelines in completing this workbook

Reading Assignment (Week 2) "Recognizing Your Spiritual Gift/s"

- Book- Growing Your Ministry God's Way: Using Your Spiritual Gifts, read pages 14-15 and meditate on these pages.
- Study Bible- Read the book of Haggai, chapters 1-2

Discussion Questions

1. DQ should be at least 150 words each.

2. In your reading assignment pages 14- 15 write the Spiritual gifts found in Romans 12:6-8, 1 Corinthians 12:7-11, Ephesians 4:11, and what does it mean to the church? Discuss it with a family member, friend, or a church member.

Share time

- In the book of Haggai identify his Spiritual gift then write at least 150 words essay and share with a family member, friend, or church member how God used him to bring glory to His name.

Reflection

- In this session the topic that we're going to go over is "Recognizing your Spiritual gift/s," and why it is important for the church (the believers in Christ Jesus) to embrace them and use them. As we see in the story of Haggai chapter 1 and 2 he certainly knew what his spiritual gifts were and used it to bring glory to the Lord. We are required to do the same.

GERTRUDE JOANNE POLLARD- WATTS

Words of Encouragement: "Consider it pure joy, my brothers, whenever you face trails of many kinds, because you know that the testing of your faith develops perseverance. Perseverance must finish its work so that you may be mature and complete, not lacking anything," James 1:1-4

Growing Your Ministry God's Way Workbook: Using Your Spiritual Gifts

Lesson 2 Note: All Quizzes are due by Friday of every Week

* This week's quiz will be focused on "The Introduction and Why God Gives Spiritual Gifts." Questions will be taken from your readings and will be given in a way that will allow one to think about the importance of why God blesses his children with Spiritual Gifts. And, applying the concepts into ones' ministry in faith, and allowing God to grow their ministry.

Week 2- Quiz

1. What are Spiritual gifts and why do we need them?

2. Can Spiritual gifts be a blessing to others? Explain.

3. What are the Spiritual gifts found in Romans 12:6-8?

4. What are the Spiritual gifts found in 1Corinthians 12:7-11?

5. What are the Spiritual gifts Ephesians 4:11?

6. There are different kinds of Spiritual gifts, all comes from?

7. True ministry is exercising the _____ of God with your Spiritual gifts.

Growing Your Ministry God's Way Workbook: Using Your Spiritual Gifts

*Lesson 3 will last for 2 Weeks

Reading Assignment (Week 3) "Understanding What Spiritual Gift/s Entails"

- Book- Growing Your Ministry God's Way: Using Your Spiritual Gifts, read pages 16-24 and meditate on these pages.
- Study Bible- Read the book of Nehemiah chapters 1-2

Discussion Questions

1. DQ should be at least 150 words each.

2. In your reading assignment pages 16-24 it explains what Spiritual gifts entails. Write then discuss with a family

member, friend or a church member two Spiritual gifts you haven't already talked about, and how understanding their concepts opens the doors of growth in the church.

<u>Notice:</u> When responding to DQ's it must be done in a Mature and Respectful way.

<u>Growing Your Ministry God's Way Workbook: Using Your Spiritual Gifts</u>

Lesson 3   <u>Note:</u> All Quizzes are due by Friday of every Week

* This week's quiz will be focused on "Understanding What Spiritual Gift's Entails." Questions will be taken from your readings and will be given in a way that will allow one to think about the importance of knowing what Spiritual Gifts are and why they are given. The quiz will also contain biblical scriptures that are quoted in your reading as well. When understanding the concept of these Spiritual gifts and applying them God's way in faith will open the door for God to bring growth to your ministry.

Week 3- Quiz

1. T/F Men and women must speak from their flesh when using the Spiritual gift of prophecy.

2. If anyone speak he/she should do it as one is speaking the very word of who?

3. What can Spiritual gifts bring forth through the ministries of God?

4. Why are some Christians not using the Spiritual gift of prophecy in modern day world?

5. What should the church should be aware of because there are many that exist in the world in which we live?

6. What does Matthew 20:28 tells us?

7. Who is the Son of Man?

8. Who make sure the needs of others become their focus in their lives and work toward meeting the needs of the receiver?

9. Is Kingdom work being done in the world today? In what ways the Spiritual gift of serving being done around the world?

10. What does the scripture tells us in Matthew 25:40?

11. Carrying the Word of God is a great responsibility. Who are given this Spiritual gift?

12. What is the Word of God must be guided by?

13. What does 2 Timothy 4:2-5 tells us to do?

14. What happens when the Word of God is carried correctly, and what happens when it's not carried correctly?

15. What does the scripture tells us in Matthew 15:14?

16. What does each letter's in the word "Bible" stands for?

17. What does Titus 2:7-8 tells preachers and teachers who teaches the Word of God?

18. What Spiritual gift uplifts the soul of a person and allows him/her to press on during lift's toughest battles?

19. What is to Spiritual gift of Encouragement can also be known as?

20. Understanding what Spiritual gifts entails does what?

Share time

- In your reading of Nehemiah chapters 1-2, write at least 150 words essay and share with a family member, friend or church member how God used Nehemiah to be a blessing to others, and point out Nehemiah's Spiritual gift/s in the essay.

Reflection

One can surely see in the book of Nehemiah chapters 1 and 2 that Nehemiah certainly had a heart for God and his father and the people in his hometown. God will always supply and open door for his children to walk through in the time of need.

Words of Encouragement: "Though he brings grief, he will show compassion, so great is his unfailing love," Lamentations 3:32

Growing Your Ministry God's Way Workbook: Using Your Spiritual Gifts

*Lesson 3 and 4 Continues (Week 4)

Reading Assignment (Week 4) "Understanding What Spiritual Gift/s Entail" con't

- Book- Growing Your Ministry God's Way: Using Your Spiritual Gifts, read pages 16-24 and meditate on these pages.

Discussion Questions

1. DQ should be at least 150 words each.

2. In your reading assignment pages 16-24 focus on where it talks about the Spiritual gift of contributing.

3. Write then discuss with a family member, friend or church member some other ways one can contribute which are not talked about in the book. Explain your answer of how it can be a blessing to the Church and the community.

*Lesson 4 (Week 4)

* This week's quiz will be a continuation from the readings of week three. The focused will still be on "Understanding What Spiritual Gift's Entails." Questions will be taken from your readings and will be given in a way that will

GROWING YOUR MINISTRY GOD'S WAY WORKBOOK

allow one to think about the importance of knowing what Spiritual Gifts are and why they are given. The quiz will also contain biblical scriptures that are quoted in your reading as well. When understanding the concept of these Spiritual gifts and applying them God's way in faith will open the door for God growing your ministry.

Note: All Quizzes are due by Friday of every Week

Week 4- Quiz

1. What Spiritual gift the pastor/teacher falls under?

2. What does Apostle Paul command to the followers in 1Thessalonians 5:12-13?

3. It will come a time where the children of God will have to show what? They must do it in what way?

4. What does James 1:5 says about the Spiritual gift of wisdom?

5. T/F the Spiritual gift of knowledge does not come from the same Spiritual gift of wisdom.

6. What does the scriptural definition of Faith?

7. Yes/No Are Christians saved by their works?

8. What does the scripture says in Ephesians 2:8?

9. Name some of the people of God in the Bible who showed great faith in the Lord.

10. In your Bible reading give an example how Jesus went about healing the sick. State the scripture and elaborate on what happened in the process.

11. T/F Even though God has given some the Spiritual gift of healing, one must remember the healing power is coming from God, through his children.

12. What can prevent the disciples of Jesus from activating their Spiritual gift of healing capabilities?

13. What does the children of God must combine with their faith when it comes to using their Spiritual gift of healing?

14. What does scripture says in Isaiah 53:5? This scripture is referring to who?

15. God blesses some of his children with the Spiritual gift of 'working miracles." What is another name for this gift?

16. The working of miracles can come in many forms. Name some ways in the Bible Jesus performed miracles.

17. There are two kinds of prophets, what are they?

28. What spiritual gift can be used to warn the children of God that false teaching is prevalent in the church?

29. What are the three things that activates the use of spiritual gifts?

20. What does 1Corinthians 14:27-28 tells us about the Spiritual gift of speaking in tongues.

21. Who is the person speaking to when he/she speaks in tongues?

22. He/she who prophesies edifies who? Where can one find this in scripture?

23. When Jesus started his ministry, he chose twelve men, what were they known as?

24. What were the roles of the twelve men?

25. If you do not know what your spiritual gift/s are who do you ask? And, John 16:13-14 says?

26. What is stated in Matthew 28:19-20?

Share time

- Read page 24 in your book and meditate on it. It tells about all the spiritual gifts God has given his children to edify his name, and to be a blessing to others. Write at least 150 words essay stating your spiritual gift and how you are using it to be a blessing to others and bring glory to God. Share it with a family member, friend, or a church member. If you have more than one spiritual gift, write about your dominant one.

Reflection

Throughout the Old Testament, and the New Testament one can see many of God's people used their spiritual gifts to bring glory to God's name. We must continue to use our spiritual gifts just the same.

Words of Encouragement: "We have different gifts, according to the grace given us. If a man's gift is prophesying, let him use it in proportion to his faith," Romans 6:12

Growing Your Ministry God's Way Workbook: Using Your Spiritual Gifts

*Lesson 5

Note: Please follow the Course Syllabus and the instructions for all guidelines of this course.

Reading Assignment (Week 5) "How to Use Your Spiritual Gift/s God's Way and Reap a Harvest in Your Ministry"

- Book- Growing Your Ministry God's Way: Using Your Spiritual Gifts read pages 25-28 meditate on these pages.
- Study Bible- Read Mark 2:1-12 name at least two key principles that are in this story.

Discussion Questions

1. DQ should be at least 150 words each.

2. In your reading assignment pages 25-28 it talks about five key principles. Write then discuss with a family member, friend, or church member these key principles and why it's necessary in discipleship.

Notice: When responding to DQ's it must be done in a Mature and Respectful way.

Growing Your Ministry God's Way Workbook: Using Your Spiritual Gifts

Note: All Quizzes are due by Friday of every Week

* This week's quiz will be focused on "How to Use Your Spiritual Gift/s God's Way and Reap a Harvest in Your Ministry." Questions will be taken from your readings and will be given in a way that will allow one to think about the importance of using their Spiritual gift/s God's way in faith and allowing God to grow their ministry.

Week 5- Quiz

1. In the beginning was the Word and the Word was with God, and the Word was God, where in scripture would you find this statement?

2. T/F praying is an action word.

3. Philippians 4:6 states, "Do not be anxious about anything, but in everything how do we present our request to the Lord?

4. T/F In order to bring about a change, one must have the love of God for God and people.

5. What do all ministries must be exercised in?

6. If God has gifted you with many spiritual gifts, but you don't have love in your heart it is worthless, what scripture is this statement referring to?

7. T/F There will be times in your ministry when you must not forgive one for wrongful behavior.

8. What does Ephesians 4:32 instructs us to do?

9. What happens if one does not forgive another for their sins?

10. When someone is experiencing trials and tribulations in their life and another person shows that they care about that person, what do you call this act?

11. What did Jesus show when he went about healing the sick and feeding the hungry?

12. What kind of words are love, forgiveness, compassion, and faith?

13. What is the definition of faith according to Hebrews 11:1?

14. Yes/No can one please God without faith? Explain.

15. Name three people of God in the Bible who show faith in God and was obedient to their calling.

16. If you are a believer in Christ Jesus do the Holy Spirit resides in you? Name a scripture which one can find this and write that scripture down.

17. What scripture tells why God sent his Holy Spirit to the believers in Christ? And write down what that scripture says.

18. What is another name for the Holy Spirit?

19. True/False all of God's children are Omnipotent, Omniscient, and Omnipresent.

20. True/False Christians may have different kinds of spiritual gift's but they all come from the same spirit and God works all of them in all men?

21. True/False the church lacks spiritual gifts.

22. Who should Christians allow to be their guide?

23. What was with God in the beginning?

24. In John 1:1 the word became what? and made his dwelling among us?

25. Who is the image of the invisible God, the firstborn over all creations?

26. Who are the head of the body, the Church?

Share time

- Secession five talks about how to use your spiritual gift/s along with key principles in growing your ministry. Write at least 250 words essay identifying these key principles and how Jesus used them in His ministry. Share it with a family member, friend or a church member.

Reflection

Jesus is the perfect model for us to follow when it comes to praying, love, forgiveness, compassion and faith. One should always reflect on Jesus' examples which he gave us in his Word when we're go through troubling times in our lives.

> *Words of Encouragement: "Blessed rather of those who hear the word of God and obey it," Luke 11:28*

Growing Your Ministry God's Way Workbook: Using Your Spiritual Gifts

*Lesson 6

Reading Assignment (Week 6) "How to Sustain One's Ministry"

- Book- Growing Your Ministry God's Way: Using Your Spiritual Gifts read pages 29-30 and meditate on these pages.
- Study Bible- Read the book of Esther. It's a great book about how the people of God can overcome destruction when one allows their focus to be on God in the mist of sorrow.

Discussion Questions

1. DQ should be at least 150 words each.

2. In your reading assignment pages 29—30, write then discuss with a family member, friend or a church member what happens when Christians make God there focus while using their Spiritual gifts.

3. When reading pages 29-30 in your reading assignment one can certainly say that Mordecai and Queen Esther had a love for God and others, what are some of the ways they showed love?

Growing Your Ministry God's Way Workbook: Using Your Spiritual Gifts

<u>Note:</u> All Quizzes are due by Friday of every Week

* This week's quiz will be focused on "How to Sustain Your Ministry." Questions will be taken from your readings and will be given in a way that will allow one to think about the importance of sustain ones' ministry in the ways of God and applying the concepts into your ministry in faith and allowing God to grow their ministry.

Week 6- Quiz

1. T/F When the people of God do not follow the will of God it hinders the blessings of the God.

2. What happens when the ministries of God are blessed?

3. What are <u>seven</u> things Christians can do to help sustain their ministry?

4. T/F Christians must always have an intimate relationship with God in prayer.

5. What does Mark 11:24 tells us about prayer?

6. What biblical scriptures states "Blessed rather are those who hear the word of God and obey it?

7. What spirit does Christians must Always Operate/Serve in?

8. T/F Mark 12:30 states that we should love the Lord with all our heart and soul period. If this is correct circle true, if it's not correct write the correct answer.

9. What is the second command in Mark 12:31?

10. In times of need Christians must look to the hills to whom for help?

Share time

Secession six talks about how to sustain one's ministry. Write at least 250 words essay identifying these key principles and how you would use them to help sustain your ministry. Share it with a family member, friend, or a church member.

Reflection

In the book of Esther, one can surely say it brings out the key principles that are needed in a ministry. Mordecai, Esther and all the Jewish people were placed in a life threating situation but their faith and trust in God allowed them to see the power of God, as He turned things around. Glory be to God!

Words of Encouragement: "And we, who with unveiled faces all reflect the Lord's glory, are being transformed into his likeness with ever-increasing glory, which comes from the Lord, who is the Spirit," 2 Corinthians 3:18

Using Your Spiritual Gifts

*Lesson 7

Reading Assignment (Week 7)

"A Blessed Ministry Brings Forth Growth in the Church"

- Book- Growing Your Ministry God's Way: Using Your Spiritual Gifts read page 31 and meditate on this page.
- Study Bible- Read Matthew 20:29-34, Mark 8:1-10, Luke 4:38-44, and John 2:1-12

Discussion Questions

1. DQ should be at least 150 words each.

2. In your reading assignment page 31, discuss with a family member, friend or church member how leading in the ways of God in faith will draw people to Jesus Christ.

3. From your Study Bible readings, name some things Jesus did to draw people to him during his ministry. Then state which one of the Gospels you got your answers.

Notice: When responding to DQ's it must be done in a Mature and Respectful way.

Growing Your Ministry God's Way Workbook: Using Your Spiritual Gifts

Note: All Quizzes are due by Friday of every Week

* This week's quiz will be focused on "How a Blessed Ministry Brings Forth Growth in the Church" Questions will be taken from your readings and will be given in a way that will allow one to think about the importance of leading in the ways of God in faith and allowing God to grow their ministry.

Week 7- Quiz

1. T/F When the church is doing the will of God it brings about blessings not only to the church but also to the community.

2. How can Christians point people to Christ Jesus for His purpose and glory?

3. In the Gospels what did God went about showing when he went about healing the sick?

4. In your reading Matthew 20:29-34, there were two blind men sitting by the roadside, and when they heard that Jesus was going by, what did they shout out loud?

5. What must the children of God exercise in God when serving in their ministry?

6. In your readings Mark 8:1-11 a large crowd had been with Jesus for three days. What did Jesus showed for them because they had not eaten? Some had come a long way.

7. Why did Jesus did not want to send a large crowd back home hungry?

8. We must always give thanks to the Lord for the blessings he gives us, what kind of food Jesus gave thanks to his Heavenly Father for the people to eat in Mark 8:1-11?

9. T/F the people ate and still was hungry because they had no more food left.

10. How many people was feed?

11. T/F after they were fed Jesus, his disciple and the people went to an unknown place the name of Dalmanutha.

12. In the readings Luke 4:38-43 a person's mother-in-law was sick with a fever, who is that person the scripture is referring to?

13. In the readings John 2:1-12 there was a wedding, what was the first miracle Jesus performed at Cana in Galilee?

14. T/F When Jesus mother informed him that the wine was depleted. He knew that his time had come.

15. In John 2:1-12 how many water jars, was used and what did the Jews used the water jars for?

16. How many gallons did the water jars hold?

17. Who told the servants to fill the jars with water?

18. T/F The water Jesus turned into wine was the best wine that was saved for last.

19. T/F When Jesus turned the water into wine this was not the first miracle Jesus performed?

20. Was the Glory of the Lord was shown at the wedding to cause the disciples to put their faith in him?

Share time

- Secession 7 talks about how "A Blessed Ministry Brings forth Growth in the Church."
  Write a 250 words essay explaining how leading in the ways of God can point people to Jesus Christ as he allows their ministry to grow. Share it with a family member, friend or a church member.

Reflection

There are many ways the Glory of God can shine through us once we allow Him to work through us. Jesus went about doing his Heavenly Father's will and healed many people. He also did many other miracles along the way in his ministry.

Words of Encouragement: "For we are his workmanship, created in Christ Jesus for good works, which God prepared in advance for us to do," Ephesians 2:10

Growing Your Ministry God's Way Workbook: Using Your Spiritual Gifts

*Lesson 8

"Thanking God in all Things"

Reading Assignment (Week 8)

- Book- Growing Your Ministry God's Way: Using Your Spiritual Gifts read page 32-33 and meditate on these pages.
- Study Bible- Read 2 Corinthians 1:1-11; and focus on verses 3 and 4.

Discussion Questions

1. DQ should be at least 150 words each.

2. In your Study Bible reading assignment verses 3 and 4, it tells why Christians should give God thanks. Write and discuss with a family member, friend, or a church member why it's important and

give an example when you applied this principle to your life and shared it with someone else.

Growing Your Ministry God's Way Workbook: Using Your Spiritual Gifts

Note: All Quizzes are due by Friday of every Week

* This week's quiz will be focused on "Thanking God in All Things" Questions will be taken from your readings and will be given in a way that will allow one to think about the importance of giving God the glory in everything in faith and allowing the peace of God to resonate in your hearts during challenging times in ones' ministry.

Week 8- Quiz

1. 1Chronicles 16:34 tells us to do what?

2. In John 16:33, Jesus told his disciples, "I have told you these things, so that in me you will have peace." What did Jesus tell them?

3. What does Paul tell us to do in 1Thessalonians 5:16-18?

4. Romans 8:38-39 states?

5. What are you thankful to God for?

Share time

- Secession 8 instructs Christians to always give thanks to God in their ministry."
  Write a 250 words essay explaining why thanking God in everything can give one a since of peace when there is trouble in their ministry. Share it with a family member, friend or a church member.

Reflections

As one journeys through some of the narratives in the bible, one will read about Jesus giving thanks to his Heavenly Father on certain occasions. He gave thanks to his heavenly father for the food they ate in Matthew 15:35-37. Also, Jesus gave thanks before instituting the Last Supper; Matthew 26:26-29. Jesus set the example for his disciples to follow, and they did as one can see in Colossians 1:1-5 the apostle Paul along with Timothy gave thanks to God in prayer for their faithful brothers in Christ at Colosse, for the love they had for all the saints… and we must also remember to thank God for all the love and kindness He gives us unconditionally.

Words of Encouragement: "Not to us, O LORD, not to us, but to your name give glory because of your lovingkindness, because of your love and faithfulness," Psalm 115:1

Growing Your Ministry God's Way Workbook: Using Your Spiritual Gifts

Lesson 9 (Assay)

Share time

- Write a 250 Word Assay telling how this course will benefit you in your ministry. Share it with a family member, friend, or a church member.

Words of Encouragement: "As long as it is day, we must do the work of him who sent me. Night is coming, when no one can work. While I am in the world, I am the light of the world," John 9:4

Now It's Time for Some Fun!

USING YOUR SPIRITUAL GIFTS

SEEK -N- FIND

(Spiritual Gifts)

D	H	E	A	L	I	N	G	Q	W	E	R	T	Y	G	S	C	J
I	K	M	E	V	P	G	N	I	T	U	B	I	R	T	N	O	C
S	B	E	J	L	W	I	S	D	O	M	B	V	I	P	S	E	S
C	K	C	N	E	S	J	O	B	H	S	E	T	L	R	O	V	E
E	N	C	O	U	R	A	G	E	K	N	I	T	E	B	H	L	G
R	O	K	B	O	E	B	W	I	A	C	L	W	V	S	X	E	N
N	W	N	P	N	A	P	E	V	A	P	O	K	A	N	O	L	O
M	L	W	R	C	R	O	T	S	A	P	V	L	N	C	U	Q	T
E	E	A	O	Z	B	D	S	E	S	R	J	B	G	I	G	S	N
N	D	B	P	N	K	I	X	U	E	A	O	Y	E	A	N	V	I
T	G	V	H	I	K	A	O	L	M	Y	N	O	L	F	U	J	G
B	E	L	E	V	I	L	O	K	N	I	F	A	I	T	H	Y	N
Z	A	I	T	J	U	K	I	C	U	N	E	W	S	Z	O	R	I
Y	Q	P	A	C	K	I	A	B	X	G	L	V	T	P	X	R	K
C	U	B	A	P	O	S	T	L	E	N	K	L	O	Z	C	O	A
R	I	R	T	R	Y	Z	R	E	H	C	A	E	T	C	A	S	E
E	I	X	V	O	P	B	I	T	S	E	R	V	I	N	G	O	P
M	L	E	A	D	E	R	S	H	I	P	O	T	E	V	O	L	S

Apostle **Faith** **Miraculous Powers**

Contributing **Healing** **Pastor** **Speaking in tongues**

Discernment **Knowledge** **Praying** **Teaching**

Encourage **Leadership** **Prophet** **Wisdom**

Evangelist **Mercy** **Serving**

"There are different kinds of gifts, but the same Spirit distributes them," 1 Corinthians 12:4 NIV.

USING YOUR SPIRITUAL GIFTS

SEEK -N- FIND

(Words Associated with Discipleship)

P	I	H	S	N	O	I	T	A	L	E	R	L	A	N	O	S	R	E	P
E	F	M	I	S	S	I	O	N	A	R	Y	E	L	F	R	P	U	I	E
L	U	F	H	T	I	A	F	K		R	C	M	K	N	E	E	B	O	J
I	O	B	E	V	S	G	N	I	Y	A	R	P	I	S	W	A	H	Y	E
V	L	V	H	O	L	Y	S	P	I	R	I	T	V	G	O	B	E	Y	R
E	P	J	E	Q	U	A	K	Z	S	E	U	X	I	N	L	P	A	W	T
R	V	E	J	A	X	G	B	I	B	L	E	M	L	I	L	E	O	J	Y
I	T	S	K	E	S	N	T	E	Z	P	W	E	J	V	O	X	L	B	U
B	N	U	K	P	O	I	Y	C	D	L	B	L	K	R	F	A	I	T	H
E	G	S	I	J	V	R	S	Z	L	O	E	P	O	E	E	K	T	E	I
L	N	C	U	K	V	A	C	T	C	U	S	I	A	S	C	N	A	K	O
I	I	R	O	Y	C	H	I	S	P	V	A	C	T	U	B	L	I	R	P
V	R	I	A	P	O	S	T	L	E	W	K	S	K	Y	E	N	O	W	Q
E	A	S	Y	Z	K	E	U	I	O	A	W	I	E	R	P	I	Z	K	E
R	C	T	L	E	A	R	N	E	R	C	N	D	I	O	U	Y	T	R	W

Apostle	**Faithful**	**Jesus Christ**	**Obey**
Bible	**Faith**	**Learner**	**Praying**
Believer	**Follower**	**Love**	**Serving**
Caring	**Healer**	**Missionary**	**Sharing**
Disciple	**Holy Spirit**	***Personal Relationship**	

"Therefore, go and make disciples of all nations, baptizing them in the name of the Father and of the Son and of the Holy Spirit, and teaching them to obey everything I have commanded you. And surely, I am with you always, to the very end of the age," Matthew 28:19-20, NIV

GROWING YOUR MINISTRY GOD'S WAY WORKBOOK

MATCH GAME

(People in the Bible)

*Match the people with their story: Example below:

John the Baptist -------------------------- Baptized Jesus

Haggai	was thrown in the lion's den
Nehemiah	vision of the valley of dry bones
Obadiah	stayed inside a great fish for 3 days and 3 nights
Jonah	prophesied the destruction of Edom
Amos	prophesied the unfaithfulness of Israel to God
Jeremiah	"prophesied the destruction of Judah by a plague of locusts that impoverished the people"
Daniel	king permitted him to rebuild the walls of Jerusalem
Hannah	married to the priest Zechariah
Elizabeth	was able to save her people from destruction
Esther	was without child
Ezekiel	led the Israelites out of Egypt
Moses	a man after God's own heart
David	the weeping prophet
Hosea	prophesied invasion of Judah & Israel & other nations
Joel	prophesied about rebuilding the temple

"Do your best to present yourself to God as one approved, a workman who does not need to be ashamed and who correctly handles the word of truth," 2 Timothy 2:15.

*Conclusion

Having a productive ministry is very important to the welfare of the church and the community in which we serve, near and abroad. God never intended for his church (the believers in Christ) to be stagnated or non-productive when it comes to serving God and pointing people to Christ Jesus. God has given everyone Spiritual gifts for the upbuilding of his kingdom and for the edification of his name. We must continue to use our Spiritual gifts and make disciples as we study the Word of God, while applying it to our lives and sharing it with others.

"Growing Your Ministry God's Way Workbook: Using Your Spiritual Gifts" shows the teachings of Jesus as he set the perfect example of how his followers should model him. Sometimes he would teach individually, "The Rich Young Ruler," Mark 10:17-27, sometimes small groups, "Jesus Walks on Water," Matthew 14:22-34, and sometime large groups, "Early Ministry in Galilee," Matthew 4:23-25. But, most of all Jesus wanted his followers to study, learn, discuss, and share the Good News about Him and make disciples. We are required to do the same.

So, as you journey through "Growing Your Ministry God's Way Workbook: Using Your Spiritual Gifts," you will find words of encouragements along the way and remember to stay anchored in Jesus Christ, who is *human and divine* and alive and well, sitting on the right-hand side of his Father in Heaven, waiting for us to cry out to Him for help when needed to do his will.

*Blessing Others

As we study the Word (Bible) we know that water is used to represent the "Word of God," and the Cleansing of Sin. So, not only does God give us water for our Spiritual needs, He also gives us water for our Physical needs. **So, please plant a seed in a charity that is giving "Water" to those who thirst around the world!**

Thank you, and may God bless you!

GERTRUDE JOANNE POLLARD-WATTS

Growing Your Ministry God's Way Workbook: Using Your Spiritual Gifts

Answer Sheet

Discussion Question

Lesson 1 Quiz- Week 1 (Answer Sheet)

1. Having a loving spirit (p.11)

2. Open answer- "your thoughts"

3. False (p.11)

4. faith (Study Bible)

5. Hebrew 11:6

6. Daniel refused to acknowledge the decree

7. Daniel prayed in faith and put his trust in God

8. A decree that anyone who prays to any god or man during the next thirty days, except King Darius shall be thrown into the lion's den. (Study Bible/Daniel 6)

9. No- because the word of God says in Exodus 20:3 "You should have no other gods before me."

10. God (p.13)

11. Yes (p.13)

12. God gives spiritual gifts to be a blessing to others and to also for kingdom building (p.13)

13. No- because some people are fearful in using them and some don't know what their spiritual gifts

14. Open answer- "your thoughts"

15. False

Lesson 2 Quiz- Week 2 (Answer Sheet)

1. Spiritual gifts are blessings that comes from the Lord and are used for his glory. God gives everyone Spiritual gift/s to edify his name, and for the building of his kingdom (p.14).
2. Open answer- "your thoughts".
3. Prophesy, serving, teaching, encouraging, contributing to the needs of others, leadership, and showing mercy (p.14)

4   The gift of wisdom, knowledge, faith, healing, miraculous powers, prophecy, discerning between spirits, speaking in tongues, interpreting tongues (p.14)

5   God give some to be apostles, prophets, evangelists, pastors, and teachers (p. 14)

6   The same spirit, and that spirit is the spirit of the Lord (p.14)

7   Principles (p.14)

Lesson 3 Quiz-Week 3 (Answer Sheet)

1. False (p.17)

2. God (p.16)

3. hope, love, unity, and disciples (p.17).

4. The gift of prophecy is looked down upon by many and it is usually quenched by the gifted one. In the eyes of some people it carries unwanted connotations (p.17).

5. false prophets (p.17)

6. "Just as the Son of Man did not come to be served, but to serve, and give his life as a ransom for many," (p.17)

7. Jesus Christ (p.17)

8. Servants of God (p.17)

9. Yes, the servants of God are feeding the hungry, giving water to the thirsty, giving shelter to the ones who don't have a place to stay, or clothes to wear, visiting the sick, and prison bound (p.17)

10. To provide the needs of the less fortunate, these brothers of mine, you did it for me (p.17)

11. Preachers and teachers (p.18)

12. the Holy Spirit (p.18)

13. Preach the Word- be prepared in season and out of season, correct, rebuke, and encourage with great patient and careful instruction (p.18).

14. When the word of God is carried correctly it points people to Christ Jesus and when it's not carried correctly it will drive people away from our Heavenly Father, or make the listeners corrupt like the carrier (p.18).

15. Leave them they are blind guides, if a blind man leads a blind man, both will fall into a pit (p.18).

16. Bible- Basic Instruction Before Leaving Earth

17. In everything set them an example by doing what is good. In your teaching show integrity, seriousness and soundness of speech that cannot be condemned, so that who oppose you may be ashamed because they have nothing bad to say about us, (p.18).

18. the spiritual gift of encouragement (p.18)

19. the spiritual gift of exhortation (p.19)

20. opens the doors to growth (p.16)

Lesson 3 and 4 Quiz - Week 4 (Answer Sheet)

1. leadership (p.19)

2. Now we ask you brothers, to respect those who work hard among you, who are over you in the Lord and who admonish you. Hold them in highest regards in love because of their work. Live in peace with each other (p.19).

3. mercy, cheerfully (p.19)

4. If any of you lacks wisdom, he should ask God, who gives generously to all without finding fault, and it will be given to him. (Study Bible)

5. False (p.20)

6. Now faith is the substance of things hoped for, and the evidence of things not seen (Hebrew 11:6)

7. No (p.21)

8. for it is by grace you have been saved, through faith, and this not from yourselves, it a gift from God, not by works (Ephesian 2:8) also p. 21 in book

9. Noah, Abraham, Jacob, Daniel, Ester, Ruth, and David (p.21).

10. Open answer "your thoughts"

11. God (p.21)

12. little faith (p.22)

13. compassion, love, and faith (p.22)

14. Jesus was "pierced for our transgressions, he was crushed for our iniquities, the punishment that brought us peace was upon him, and by his wounds we are healed (p.22)

15. spiritual gift of miraculous powers (p.22)

16. Open answer "your thoughts"

17. There are true prophets and false prophets (p.22)

18. the spiritual gift of discernment (p.22)

19. Holy Spirit, Faith, and the love for Christ Jesus, and his children (p.23)

20. "If anyone speaks in a tongue, two- or at the most three-should speak one at a time, and someone must interpret. If there is no interpreter the speaker should keep quiet in the church and speak to himself and God," 1 Corinthians 14:27-28, also (p.23)

21. the person is speaking directly to God (p.23)

22. edifies the Church, 1 Corinthians 14:4, also (p.23)

23. the twelve apostles, (p.23)

24. they were to equip the saints for service and edify the body of the church. (p.23)

25. Ask God to allow his Holy Spirit to reveal it to you… And John 16:13-14 states, "But when the Spirit of truth comes, he will guide you into all truth. He will not speak on his own; he will speak only what he hears, and he will tell you what is yet to come. He will bring glory to me by taking from what is mine and making it known to you." (p.24)

26. "Therefore go and make disciples of all nations, baptizing them in the name of the father, and of the Son, and of the Holy Spirit, teaching them to obey everything I have commanded you, and surly I am with you always to the very end of age." (p.23)

Lesson 5 Quiz- Week 5 (Answer Sheet)

1. John 1:1-2 (p.25)

2. True (p.25)

3. Prayer, and petition, with thanksgiving (p.26)

4. T/F In order to bring about a change, one must have the love of God for God and people. (p.26)

5. Love (p.26)

6. 1Corinthains 13:1-3 (p.26)

7. False (p.26)

8. Ephesians 4:32 instructs us to be kind and compassionate to one another, and forgiving each other, just as Christ God forgave you. (p.26)

9. Our Heavenly Father will not forgive us (p.26)

10. Showing compassion (p.27)

11. Jesus showed compassion (p.27)

12. Action words (p.27)

13. Hebrews 11:1 state, "Faith is the things hope for, and the evidence of things not seen. (p.27)

14. No, because Hebrew 11:6 states "And without faith it is impossible to please God, because anyone who comes to him must believe that he exists and rewards those who earnestly seek him." (p.27)

15. Noah, Abraham, Isaac, Jacob, Moses etc.

16. Yes, 1Corinthians 6:19 states "Do you not know that your body is a temple of the Holy Spirit, who is in you, whom you have received from God?"

17. Our Heavenly Father sent it, John 14:26 states "But the Counselor, the Holy Spirit, whom the Father will send in my name, will teach you all things and will remind you of everything I have said to you (p.28).

The Counselor (John 14:26; p28), (Note: can be other names, just state the scripture where you got it from)

18. False (p.28)

19. True

20. False (p.28)

21. The Holy Spirit (p.28)

22. The Word (p.28)

23. flesh (p.28)

24. Jesus (p28)

25. Jesus Christ (p28)

Lesson 6 Quiz- Week 6 (Answer Sheet)

1. True (p.29)

2. it thrives (p.29)

3. Christians must first and for most make God the center of their ministry, have a prayer line open to God, keep their eyes on Jesus, listen to the words God as he instructs you along the way, keep your heart and mind on Jesus and block/cancel out anything that is not of God, always

operate your ministry in the spirit of love, and pray and look to God for help (p.29-30)

4. True (p.29)

5. Mark11:24, "Devote yourselves to prayer, being watchful and thankful," and therefore I tell you, whatever you ask for in prayer, believe that you have received it, and it will be yours" (p.29)

6. Luke 11:28 (p.29)

7. Love (p.30)

8. False, Mark 12:30 states "Love the Lord your God with all your heart and with all your soul and with all your mind and with all your strength (p.30)

9. The second command in Mark 12:31 is "Love your neighbor as yourself" (p.30)

10. the Lord (p.30)

Lesson 7 Quiz- Week 7 (Answer Sheet)

1. True (p.31)

2. Christians can point people to Jesus by using their spiritual gifts in kingdom building for the glory of God (p.31)

3. Love and compassion (p.31)

USING YOUR SPIRITUAL GIFTS

4. "Lord, Son of David, have mercy on us!" (Matthew 20:31)

5. Their faith (p.31)

6. Compassion (Mark 8:1-11)

7. Because in fear they might collapse (Mark 8:1-11)

8. Bread and fish (Mark 8:1-11)

9. False (Mark 8:1-11)

10. About 4000 men were fed (Mark 8:1-11)

11. True

12. Luke 4:38-43 (Simon)

13. Jesus turned the water into wine (John 2:1-12)
14. False

15. There were 6 stone water jars which was used for ceremonial washing (John 2:1-12)

16. Twenty to thirty gallons (John 2:1-12)

17. Jesus (John 2:1-12)

18. True

19. False

20. Yes

Lesson 8 Quiz- Week 8 (Answer Sheet)

1. 1Chronicles 16:34 tells us to give thanks to the Lord for he is good; and his love endures forever! (p.32)

2. So that in him (Jesus) we may have peace (p.32)

3. In 1Thessalonians 5:16-18 Paul tells us to be joyful always, pray continually, give thanks in all circumstances for this is God's will for you in Christ Jesus. (p.32)

4. Romans 8:38-39 states "For I am convinced that neither death nor life, neither angels nor demons, neither the present nor the future, nor depth, nor anything else in all creation will be able to separate us from the love of God that is in Christ Jesus our Lord.

5. What are you thankful to God for?

USING YOUR SPIRITUAL GIFTS

Match Game/ Answer Sheet

(People in the Bible)

*Matching the people with their story:

John the Baptist --- Baptized Jesus

Haggai--- prophesied about rebuilding the temple

Nehemiah---king permitted him to rebuild the walls of Jerusalem

Obadiah---prophesied the destruction of Edom

Jonah--stayed inside a great fish for 3 days and 3 nights

Amos---prophesied invasion of Judah & Israel & other nations

Joel--- "prophesied the destruction of Judah by a plague of locusts that impoverished the people"

Daniel---was thrown in the lion's den

Hannah---was without child

Elizabeth---was married to the priest Zechariah

Esther---was able to save her people from destruction

Ezekiel---vision of the valley of dry bones

Moses---led the Israelites out of Egypt

David---a man after God's own heart

Hosea--- prophesied the unfaithfulness of Israel to God

End of Course Questionnaire

- Critiquing: Growing Your Ministry God's Way Workbook: Using Your Spiritual Gifts. Please take the time and email your answers to the questions to: gjpwatts.teach@gmail.com
- Note: In the future one will be able to answer the questions via website, and the iphone.

Questions:

1. Was the workbook structured in a way that was easily followed?

2. Did the workbook meet your expectations?

3. Did the workbook make you think about what you can do to enhance your ministry?

4. Was the workbook challenging?

5. Was the workbook supplies sufficient for the program?

6. Did the workbook point out the importance of Growing Your Ministry God's Way?

7. Did the workbook make in impact in your life?

8. Are you likely to recommend this workbook to someone else?

9. Did the workbook make you want to get involved in the church and use your Spiritual gift/s?

10. Was the workbook enjoyable?

11. Was the workbook designed appropriately for the book "Growing Your Ministry God's Way: Using Your Spiritual Gifts?

12. How did you hear about this workbook?

13. Was there answers provided to the test in the workbook?

14. Did words of encouragement help you alone the way?

15. Would you recommend this workbook to be used in ministries in the church?

*Note: Also, please email any concerns or suggestions that will enhance Growing Your Ministry God's Way Workbook: Using Your Spiritual Gifts to gjpwatts.teach@gmail.com

* Please take time and write a customer review about the workbook on either amazon.com, barnsandnobles.com or walmart.com

Thank you kindly, and may God bless you!

About the Author

Gertrude Joanne Pollard- Watts Sunday school teacher/ Author "Growing Your Ministry God's Way Workbook: Using Your Spiritual Gifts, writes Christian faith base/ and Inspirational books for the glory of God. She attended Grand Canyon University and earned a Bachelor of Arts degree in Christian Studies as well as a Masters' degree in Christian Studies with an emphasis in Pastoral Ministry. Once again Gertrude enrolled in college to earn a Doctor of Education (Ed. D.) degree in Organizational Leadership with emphasis in Christian Ministry, but after a year into the program Pollard-Watts withdrew from her studies and answered her calling from God to write her first book "Growing Your Ministry God's Way: Using Your Spiritual Gifts." Gertrude Watts is a member of the Tabernacle Baptist Church- West in -Evans, Georgia where she is actively involved in the Prayer Ministry, Bible Study, Adult/ Women Sunday school Ministry and the Circles of Growth Small Groups Ministry. Gertrude enjoys writing, walking/jogging in the park, and teaching and meditating on the word of God.

Thank you God.

A page for your thoughts

www.ingramcontent.com/pod-product-compliance
Lightning Source LLC
Chambersburg PA
CBHW071414290426
44108CB00014B/1818